100 Prayers George Floyd did not pray

Anthony Albert

DEDICATION

This book is dedicated to the generations that saw 8mins 45 secs of the horrific human sacrifice of George Floyd on video and was repulsed enough to spark a worldwide protest for weeks

CONTENTS

1 I WILL NOT DIE BEFORE MY GREATNESS APPEARS

Psa 7:9 Oh let the wickedness of the wicked come to an end; but establish the just: for the righteous God trieth the hearts and reins.

2Co 8:9 For ye know the grace of our Lord Jesus Christ, that, though he was rich, yet for your sakes he became poor, that ye through his poverty might be rich.

Rom.8:2 For the law of the Spirit of life in Christ Jesus hath made me free from the law of sin and death.

Irony par excellence! His Gofundme page grossed about $15m. But he died from a trouble started with a fake $20. Everybody has come to know George Floyd and his last statements, but he could not be known while alive. Everything he dreamt while alive only came to be upon his death. The grave has "swallowed down riches"! This is the nightmare of deliverance ministers on deliverance ground. All things being equal, all souls made from the very private breath of God, the Omnipotent, are unique enough to be celebrated.

As a beneficiary of the goodness of the Lord and with my humble knowledge of the word, ways and means of God, George Floyd couldn't but have been born great and lived great. In simple terms, George Floyd was born great but the greatness was swallowed up the wickedness of man and the wickedness of his foundation. And to have a glory so marvelous at death means life should also have been glorious. But it was not. Classical story of man, especially the blackman, repeating itself over and over again. The unsung glories litter the history of mankind. The soul of man, made from the very private and personal breath of God, the Omnipotent, is nothing less than great. I cannot be made in the image of God and not be great. "Born great but tied down" is the title of a book I have found relevant to the subject matter. How so true and pertinent, looking at the play out of events since the death of George Floyd. An event that looks programmed for post-Covid-19 pandemic environment. He was not the first black to be choked to death in the hands of a law enforcement agent. He was not the first to moan "I CAN'T BREATHE!" But George Floyd moaning became a battle cry to rouse up the sense of justice of mankind. Forcing a universal response to a universal multi-generational wickedness perpetrated on the black race everywhere. No matter where you turn, the lot of the black man has been nothing but disdain.

With hindsight being 20/20, regular, normal prayers would hardly be of help for George Floyd. Whenever we speak of advanced spiritual warfare, violence and aggression are requirements. There can be no negotiation with the powers that wants you tied down, though heaven is calling you great.

Strange situations will require strange prayers to get resolved. The life and death of George Floyd was strange. You need strange prayers like below to handle strange situations. A well balanced understanding of the enemy of the soul of man is a requirement for advanced spiritual warfare. Except you have the enemy knowledgeably and spiritually defined, you cannot conquer the enemy.

To die in the hand of another man, spiritually speaking, is nothing but a human sacrifice. Not to die a natural death is classified in advanced spiritual warfare as a human sacrifice. A human sacrifice in broad daylight, caught on video, is the death of George Floyd. We all saw on video, the death of George Floyd. Every sacrifice would require an altar and every altar has a Priest. Major and minor priests. The altar, the human sacrifice, and the officiating priests were all present after 3 months lockdown feast called covid-19 pandemic. Jesus has died as a sacrifice just so that no one else of the human race should die as a human sacrifice.

The use of the term "die" in the prayers below simply means, "be separated from me" as death signify the separation of the soul and the body at death. It is a spiritual warfare language commonly used in prayer battles on deliverance ground. Take these prayers if you are afraid of tomorrow. Take these prayers if your situation appears stubborn. Take these prayers if you find it difficult to make a headway in life. Take these prayers if your lot must be different from that of George Floyd. Take these prayers if you do want to go down like George Floyd. But please you must do with violence, aggression and determination on your prayer altar. Shall we war!

100 Prayers George Floyd did not pray!

1.   Jesus Christ died in the hands of the wicked as a sacrifice, I will not die in the hands of man as a human sacrifice, in the name of Jesus. (2Cor.8:9)

2.   I will not die before my glory appears, in the name of Jesus.

3.   My glory will not die in the hands of the wicked before the manifestation of my destiny, in the name of Jesus.

4.   The glory of the sun is one and the glory of the moon is another. The powers, God did not give my glory but want my glory, let my glory destroy you, in the name of Jesus.

5.   "But the wicked shall be cut off from the earth, and the transgressors shall be rooted out of it." Proverbs 2:22 KJV   I refuse to die in the hands of the wicked, satanically ordained to take my life, in the name of Jesus.

6.   I will not touch the world only in the grave, in the name of Jesus.

7.   Blood of Jesus, let the will of God be done in my life, marriage and career and let my will die, in the name of Jesus.

8.   Battles of "born great but tied down", Holy Spirit, let the battles cease in the name of Jesus.

9.   "Tear down their altars!" So it is written, dark altars that condemn men to ignominy in my father's house, I tear you down in the name of Jesus.

10. Dark altar put up to use me as human sacrifice, O God arise and let the altar die with the satanic priest on the altar in the name of Jesus.

11. Knowledge, wisdom and understanding, protected from me, that I may not access the next level in life, marriage and career, be released unto me in the name of Jesus.

12. I bring the blood of Jesus to expel every power that will not let my pride die, in the name of Jesus.

13. Powers that have no business complaining why I should be great, shut up and die and let me be great while alive, in the name of Jesus.

14. Every evil promissory note that has come up for payment in my bloodline, take the sacrifice of Christ, release me and let me live, in the name of Jesus.

15. The idols of my father, the idols of my mother, die and let my glory shine, in the name of Jesus.

16. The idols that did not allow my father to prosper in life, marriage and career, let my destiny become fire unto you, in the name of Jesus.

17. The idols that followed my parents into marriage, die and release my marriage in the name of Jesus.

18. The powers that separated my parents, I have come to Christ and my story must be different, leave my glory alone, in the name of Jesus.

19. Powers seating on my greatness, somersault and die in the name of Jesus.

20. The captivity of my father's house, the captivity of mother's house be thou removed from my life in the name of Jesus.

21. Battles of "like father like son" keeping me from greatness, expire in the name of Jesus.

22. Whosoever the son has set free is free indeed. Every prison of problems with no solution die and release me in the name of Jesus. (John 8:36)

23. The greatness that can only manifest in the grave, I reject you, reject me in the name of Jesus.

24. Who manipulated my destiny so that my greatness can only appear in the grave, die and release my destiny in the name of Jesus.

25. Strange powers feeding on my destiny like food, I riot against you and break free in the name of Jesus.

26. My Father in heaven, whenever I stand at the edge of a big loss, let the loss be prevented in the name of Jesus.

27. Barriers to greatness because of my color and race, scatter because of the cross of Christ, in the name of Jesus.

28. Limitations placed on me because of my race, scatter and die in the name of Jesus.

29. The level I cannot achieve just because I am black, Holy Spirit take me there and over in the name of Jesus.

30. Powers getting mad every time I am about to breakthrough, die and let me through in the name of Jesus.

31. Powers in my foundation to make my helpers hate and reject me, let the powers die in the name of Jesus.

32. The witchcraft that affected my parents, release me and die in the name of Jesus.

33. Dark altars that stopped my parents from greatness and are now stopping me, collapse, die and release me in the name of Jesus.

34. Powers saying because nobody ever attended college in my father's house I cannot, die and release my glory, in the name of Jesus.

35. My glory in the cage of collective captivity of my father's house, break loose by fire in the name of Jesus.

36. Failure to obey God, programmed into my life at conception, scatter and die in the name of Jesus.

37. Incapacity to love God with all my heart, soul and mind, programmed into my life at conception, die in the name of Jesus.

38. Every part of me that wants to sin, die without me in the name of Jesus.

39. I am the bride of the God that never fails. Every garment of frustration and failure put upon me, be set ablaze in the name of Jesus.

40. Every part of me that wants to pull me into the grave before my time, die without me in the name of Jesus.

41. The glory that can only shine in the grave, I reject you, reject me in the name of Jesus.

42. Strange taste and strange appetite inherited from my parents, die, in the name of Jesus.

43. Collective captivity of my father's house assigned to kill me before I become great, scatter unto destruction in the name of Jesus.

44. Lord Jesus, You called Lazarus out of the grave, call me out of failure and darkness.

45. They have eyes but they cannot see, they that make them are like unto them. Every desire of my heart that has become an idol in order to rob me of my sight and vision, perish now! In the name of Jesus.

46. They have mouth, they cannot speak, they that make them are like unto them! Idols in my heart shutting my mouth when I need to speak, perish! In the name of Jesus.

47. They have ears they cannot hear. They that make them are like unto them. Idols in my heart that will not allow me to hear from God, die! in the name of Jesus.

48. My inner man! Why are you sleeping? Wake up! in the name of Jesus.

49. If I am doing things heaven has ordained I should not do, mercy of God in Christ, stop it now.

50. Holy Spirit show me myself and decode my life/my situation, in the name of Jesus.

51. Evil pronouncements and curses that have tied me down where I do not belong, break! in the name of Jesus.

52. The promise made by my parents that have become the promise I cannot pay, sacrifice of Christ settle it now, in the name of Jesus.

53. Parental and ancestral promissory note I cannot pay, let the sacrifice of Christ redeem it and set me free, in the name of Jesus.

54. I apply to the mercy of God in Christ that saw it fit to call me into existence, let the power of great mistake in my life, marriage and career die in the name of Jesus.

55. I subscribe to your mercy O Lord, let your will be done in my life, marriage and career and let my will die in the name of Jesus.

56. I subscribe to the mercy of God in Christ Jesus, let satanic opposition to my destiny fulfillment die in the name of Jesus.

57. Battles of those wrongly claiming I have offended them, let the battles die in the name of Jesus.

58. Attacks from those wrongly claiming I have offended them, backfire in the name of Jesus.

59. Every stronghold that must scatter before I can enter into greatness, scatter now in the name of Jesus.

60. My soul magnify the Lord at all times and let my greatness appear.

61. Battles of missing virtues in my life, marriage and career, cease in the name of Jesus.

62. The courtship of my parents that was anti-kingdom, release my glory and let the prosper in the name of Jesus.

63. If my parents were not legally married before God, I am now in Christ, let the blood of Jesus break every curse of illegitimate birth upon my life in the name of Jesus.

64. Blood of Jesus break every curse of illegitimate birth assigned to tie me down in the name of Jesus.

65. If what I am called is the power blocking my progress, let the power die in the name of Jesus.

66. If my name is the power behind my problems, let the power die and let the problems die in the name of Jesus.

67. Powers with the keys to the mystery of my name, hand them over to the Holy Spirit now in the name of Jesus.

68. Lord Jesus exercise your lordship over the process that gave me a name.

69. Every thought put in my mind to make me lose the power to process my destiny assignments, I reject you, in the name of Jesus.

70. Powers generating evil thoughts and imaginations in me to have me polluted, O God arise and let the powers die, in the name of Jesus.

71. Holy Spirit, let Spirit of broken homes in my life, marriage and career die in the name of Jesus.

72. Loneliness that has become a trap to swallow my glory, I dismantle your altar in the name of Jesus.

73. Power of evil thrones tying me down, let the power be destroyed in the name of Jesus.

74. Marriage destroyers that are busy on my bloodline, O God the owner of marriage, let them die in the name of Jesus.

75. Marriage killers in my father's house, take a look at the Cross of Christ, release my marriage and die in the name of Jesus.

76. Spirit of polygamy inherited from my father, abandon your rage in my life, marriage and career in the name of Jesus.

77. Evil thrones that are anchoring failure in my life, marriage and career, scatter in the name of Jesus.

78. O Lord reveal unto me the secrets of the seasons of my life I need to know, in the name of Jesus.

79. The idol that uses ritual sex, sexual immorality to cage and knock down in my blood line, blood of Jesus let the idol die in the name of Jesus.

80. Powers using sex as an altar to sacrifice my breakthroughs, my blessings and my progress in life, die suddenly in the name of Jesus.

81. The altar using my need to call me out of Christ and get me angry, collapse and die in the name of Jesus.

82. Powers using my need to summon me into crime, O Lord let the power die and release me in the name of Jesus.

83. The altar that is saying that the sacrifice of Christ is not enough for me, let the altar collapse and die in the name of Jesus.

84. Every satanic promissory note issued on my behalf by my ancestors and its keeping me in poverty, be revoked by the power in the blood of Jesus, in the name of Jesus.

85. Thou power of strange gods legislating against my destiny, scatter, in the name of Jesus.

86. Every agenda of darkness, using my foundation to waste my life, die! In the name of Jesus.

87. My root, my foundation, let me go as it is divinely written of me! In the name of Jesus.

88. Blood of Jesus, silence every negative voice in my bloodline insisting that I cannot rise above my root.

89. If I am ignorantly asking for what will disgrace and destroy me, Holy Spirit turn down my request in the name of Jesus.

90. Everything I am looking back to with regret, by the mercy of God become my stepping stone to the next level in the name of Jesus.

91. Battles of darkness that are sponsoring wrong choices and decisions in my life, O God arise and let the battles die, in the name of Jesus.

92. If I am not so positioned that you may fight my battles, O Lord reposition me now and fight my battles, in the name of Jesus.

93. Strange battles assigned to waste my life, die! In the name of Jesus.

94. Idols of my father, idols of my mother at work in my life that I may suffer, die in the name of Jesus.

95. The curse of illegitimate birth that is keeping me from coming to Christ and prospering in Christ, blood of Jesus break the curse in the name of Jesus.

96. The battles that did not allow me to have a father, die and let me be a father, in the name of Jesus.

97. O heaven of heavens arise and interrupt the witchcraft and the wickedness of those that hate my existence, in the name of Jesus.

98. This calls for wisdom. If anyone has insight, let him calculate the number of the beast, for it is man's number. His number is 666." Rev...13:18 Holy Spirit calculate the number of my enemies and give me their secrets in the name of Jesus.

99. Bewitching pride of my heart stop working, I must love God with all my heart, soul and mind, in the name of Jesus.

100. Cast me not away from your presence O Lord and take not your Holy Spirit away from me. Holy Ghost overshadow me to make me who God created me to be and do what God created me to do, in the name of Jesus.

Each of these prayers can become a prayer program to develop more prayers if enabled by the Holy Spirit. For we know not how to pray, the way we ought, but the Holy Spirit, with groanings which cannot be uttered, makes intercessions for us. Aggressive and violent prayer battles must be engaged to avoid the fate of George Floyd. Matthew 11:12 **KJV**: And **from the days of John the Baptist** until now the kingdom of heaven suffereth violence, and the violent take it by force

To close, what would it have been like for George Floyd, if the following prayers below were available for him and his family as Christians?

The Prayers George Floyd's father as Priest of the house should have prayed.
: by George Floyd's conception
: while George Floyd was in the womb
: on the day George Floyd was born
: on the day he was given a name
: on the day George Floyd turned 1, 3, 7, 12, 13, 17, 21 years old
: on the day he became a man.

But the parents were separated. The lot of the black man is a difficult and dicey one. Battles of the unparented is ravaging the black community and consequently it is ravaging mankind.

The Christian prayer culture calls for "pray without ceasing". If the foundation be destroyed what can the righteous do? I dare to answer, the righteous can pray appropriating the grace released because of the Cross of Christ.

www.ingramcontent.com/pod-product-compliance
Lightning Source LLC
Chambersburg PA
CBHW071808020426
42331CB00008B/2441